Kimberley and
Nathan Nichols.
1992.

GW00854761

A First Guide to
Making Models

A FIRST GUIDE TO
MAKING MODELS

DIANA CRAIG

Oxford University Press

A QUARTO BOOK

Published by
Oxford University Press, Walton Street, Oxford OX2 6DP
Oxford New York Toronto Delhi Bombay Calcutta Madras Karachi
Petaling Jaya Singapore Hong Kong Tokyo Nairobi Dar Es Salaam Cape Town

and associate companies in Berlin Ibadan

Oxford is a trade mark of Oxford University Press

Copyright © 1992 Quarto Publishing plc

All rights reserved. This publication may not be reproduced, stored, or
transmitted in any forms or by any means, except in accordance with the
terms of licenses issued by the Copyright Licensing Agency, or except for fair
dealing for the purposes of research or private study, or criticism or review, as
permitted under the Copyright, Designs and Patents Act, 1988. Enquiries
concerning reproduction outside those terms should be addressed to the
Permissions Department, Oxford University Press.

A catalogue record for this book is available from the British Library.

ISBN 0 19 910044 6

This book was designed and produced by
Quarto Publishing plc
The Old Brewery, 6 Blundell Street, London N7 9BH

Creative Director Nick Buzzard
Senior Editor Cynthia O'Brien
Editors Susanne Haines, Dorothea Hall
Designers Hugh Schermuly, Julie Adams
Design Assistant Trish Going
Photographers Ian Howes, Les Weiss, Paul Forrester
Illustrator Ann Savage

The Publishers would like to thank the following for their help in the
preparation of this book: Abigail Frost, Sarah Risley, Karen Ball

The Publishers would also like to give special thanks to Maggie Rogers and
the students of Goldsmith College Design Studies Department who prepared all the projects

Typeset by En to En Typesetters, Tunbridge Wells, Kent
Manufactured in Singapore by Eray Scan Pte. Ltd.
Printed in Hong Kong

CONTENTS

MODEL-MAKING

There are so many ways to make models. In this book you will find all sorts of ideas for making models from clay and other modelling materials, from papier mâché, from paper and from junk. The photographs show you how to make the model, and the illustrations will give you some other ideas. Use your imagination, and make your ideas come to life!

PREPARE YOURSELF

Read through the instructions for the model you are making, and get together everything you need before you start to work so you can just settle down and enjoy what you are doing.

Try to find somewhere to work where you can be comfortable and can get on with your work without being disturbed, or disturbing others.

Make sure that you cover your work table with either newspaper or a plastic tablecloth to protect it, and wear an apron or overalls to keep yourself clean.

10

WHILE YOU WORK

Some clay models have to be stored under plastic or a damp cloth to prevent them from drying out if you have to leave the work in the middle.

Be patient and let the stages of the model dry or cool down before going on to painting and varnishing.

Always use non-toxic paints, glues and varnishes.

When you finish with tools that will need washing later, leave them to soak in a bowl of soapy water while you go on working so that they will be easier to clean.

If you need to use sharp knives or pliers for any of the models, always ask an adult to help you.

CLEARING UP

When you have finished, clear up everything. Throw away newspaper or, if you have been working on a plastic cloth or tabletop, wipe this down. Look out for bits and pieces that might have fallen on the floor – little blobs of plasticine or other sticky stuff can be almost impossible to remove if someone walks on them.

Wash paintbrushes in cool, soapy water, and rinse. Leave them to dry with the brush ends up (if you leave a brush with the end down, the end will become bent). Put the tops on paint pots and pens. Wash your hands, too.

Leave your models to dry somewhere out of the way, where they will be safe and not cause problems for other people.

Self-hardening clay

Marzipan

Flour

Playdough

MODELLING MATERIALS

Modelling materials are soft clay-like materials that can be built up and shaped with your hands and tools into the form that you want. They include playdough, plasticine, self-hardening clay, oven-baked clay, potter's clay, and even edible materials like pastry and marzipan.

Plasticine

Modelling tools

Oven-baked clay

Varnish

Acrylic paints

Poster paints

On pages 14 to 15 you can read about the main types of modelling materials that you can buy or make, and find out which are best for different types of model-making, but don't worry if you don't have exactly the one you want – most models can be made out of more than one material. On pages 16 to 23 the main techniques of working with these materials are described.

Paintbrushes

Garlic press

Pastry cutters

Rolling pin

Kitchen knife

SELF-HARDENING CLAY is strengthened with nylon. It is usually a pale grey colour, although there is a white one and a brown one that looks like potter's clay. It can be used to make very strong models and objects. Keep your model damp by covering it with plastic until it is finished. When joining pieces, score and dampen them. The clay will harden when left to dry in the air. It can then be painted and varnished.

CLAYS AND DOUGHS

There are a lot of different types of soft clay-like modelling materials and each one is suitable for working in a particular way and for making certain types of models. There are even some materials that you can make at home. All these clays and doughs should be stored in an airtight container, such as a plastic bag, to keep them moist. You will need a collection of modelling tools, and also some paints and varnishes.

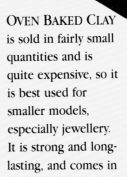

OVEN BAKED CLAY is sold in fairly small quantities and is quite expensive, so it is best used for smaller models, especially jewellery. It is strong and long-lasting, and comes in a range of bright colours. The clay is soft and pliable until it is baked in an oven. The clay dries hard once it has cooled. You can then varnish it.

PLASTICINE is very easy to use and quite cheap to buy. Once it has been modelled, plasticine keeps its shape but it does not harden so it can be used over and over again. It is not very strong, so it is not good for making things that are going to be used or worn. It comes in different colours which can be mixed together. Plasticine is also very useful modelling material for making moulds for papier mâché.

PLAYDOUGH is a very soft modelling dough that can be used to make models that do not need to have much detail. It is usually sold in tubs or packets of different colours which can be mixed together. You can make your own playdough (see the recipe) and mix your own colours by adding food colouring. If the dough becomes dry, cover it with a damp cloth overnight. Playdough models dry hard.

POTTER'S CLAY is a natural earth clay which is good for large strong models, but it must be 'fired' (or baked) in a special oven called a kiln. Before using the clay you must make sure that there are no air bubbles in it. To do this, slap the clay down on the work surface and then knead it well. Clay models should

MAKE YOUR OWN PLAYDOUGH

- 200g (7 oz) plain flour
- 100g (4 oz) salt
- 1 tablespoon oil
- 2 teaspoons cream of tartar
- a little food colouring
- 300ml (half-pint) water

Put the first four ingredients into a saucepan. Mix the food colouring with the water, and pour it into the saucepan.

Heat the mixture over medium heat, stirring all the time. Turn the mixture out on to a greased board. When it has cooled a little knead it until it becomes smooth and stretchy, but be very careful as it may still be hot inside. Soak the saucepan to stop the leftover dough from sticking to the sides.)

MAKE YOUR OWN SALTDOUGH

Saltdough is hard enough to make small models, which must be baked in the oven.
Follow the recipe below:

- 300g (10 oz) plain flour
- 300g (10 oz) salt
- 1 tablespoon oil
- 200ml (third-pint) water

1 Place all the ingredients in a bowl and mix. The mixture should feel smooth and stretchy. If it doesn't, add a little more water.

2 Turn it out on to a floured board and knead until smooth.
Place small models on a greased tray and

bake at gas mark 4/350°F (180°C) for about 10-20 minutes. Bigger models need to be baked more slowly overnight at gas mark ½/250°F (130°C). You can either add food colouring when you make it, or colour it after baking with paint or felt-tipped pens.

always be hollow or they may explode in the kiln. If you want to join new wet clay to partly dried-out clay, you must stick them together with slip (clay soaked in water to make a creamy liquid). You must leave the clay to dry out well before it is fired. When it is cool you can paint it.

TOOLS don't have to be bought from shops (although a set of plastic modelling tools will come in handy). You will find a lot of useful things in the kitchen. A rolling pin is useful, or you could use a straight-sided glass (or for small pieces, a pen). Pastry cutters, jars or glasses are good for cutting out shapes.

Use a garlic press to make strands of 'hair'. Blunt kitchen knives are useful, and forks can be used for making patterns in clay.

FLATWORK

Flat models are the easiest to make: all you do is roll out the modelling material to the thickness you want, and then cut out your models with a cutter or knife. The modelling material should be firm: oven-baked clay, self-hardening clay, plasticine and saltdough are all good, but playdough is a bit too soft to hold its shape well.

Your models should be flat at the bottom and rolled out thickly to stand up.

1 Roll out the material to the thickness you want. Try to get it an even thickness all through, and keep the edges smooth.

4 If you are using oven clay or plasticine, you can make multi-coloured models. Just roll different-coloured strips together.

NOAH'S ARK

These drawings will give you some ideas for making your own flat models. You could make pairs of animals for your own Noah's ark. Draw the shapes of the animals on a piece of card and cut out with scissors, then place the shapes on the clay and cut around the outline with a knife. Cut neatly into corners.

You could make the animals into badges by sticking a pin (or 'brooch back') onto the back with glue (see page 24).

If you want the shapes to stand up, roll out the modelling material thickly and make sure that the bottom of the design is flat. You could turn your flat models into pendants like the smiling face, by making a hole at the top and threading it with a shoe lace or piece of string.

2 Cut out shapes with a biscuit cutter. If you don't have a cutter in the shape or size you want, make a template from card, and use that as a guide to cut around.

3 These letters were cut with a special cutter. But you could just as easily cut them using a template you have made yourself.

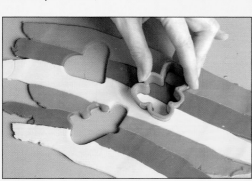

5 Cut out your models, making sure that you place the cutter across the different colours so that you get a good 'striped' effect.

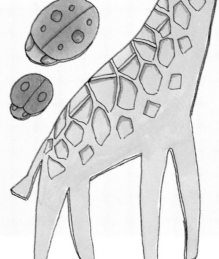

- Modelling material
- Rolling pin
- Knife
- Ruler

SLABWORK

You can build boxes and other three-dimensional models by rolling out sheets or slabs of modelling material as you did for making flat models, and joining them together. Any firm, strong modelling material will do: you can even use plasticine if you roll it fairly thick.

1 Roll out the modelling material (the slabs here are made of strips of different-coloured plasticine, rolled together). To get an even thickness, it helps to roll the pin along two matching lengths of wood. Make sure the material is thick enough to stand.

FROM BOXES TO CASTLES

You can make boxes of any shape or colour, with a lid to fit. The same method can be used to make something more ambitious like this castle. Plan all the pieces in card first, cut out the clay slabs, then make holes for windows and put on the stone decoration before joining the pieces. The larger the object, the thicker your slab will have to be.

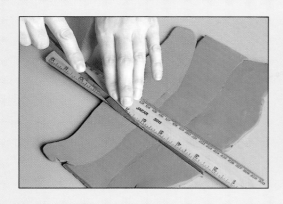

2 Cut out a square slab to form the base of your box. Cut four slabs for the sides. The length will depend on the thickness of the slabs and the way you join the pieces. The height should be the same (use a ruler or a card template to cut around).

3 Join the first side, lining it up neatly with the edge. (If you are using self-hardening clay, moisten the joining edges.) Position the second piece in place and trim the length if necessary.

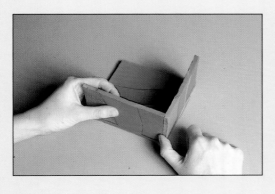

4 Join the second side to the base and the first side, smoothing the join with your fingers to neaten it.

5 Add the third and fourth sides, trimming them to fit and smoothing over any rough edges to make sure that the joins are strong.

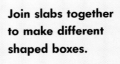

Join slabs together to make different shaped boxes.

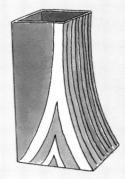

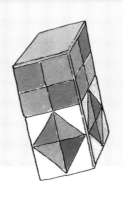

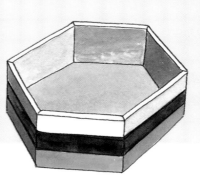

MODELLING MATERIALS

■ Modelling material

PINCHING

The easiest way to make bowls and cups is by 'pinching out' balls of modelling material. The basic method is shown on the opposite page. To make a finished pot you would need to neaten the top edges of the pot. If the base of the pot is left rounded, it will roll slightly. You can flatten it by pressing it gently on a flat surface. You can use any type of modelling material for this technique.

1 Take a handful of the modelling material and roll it roughly into a ball on the table, then roll it in the palms of your hands until the ball is well rounded and the clay is soft and workable.

Do not take too big a handful of modelling material otherwise it may be too much for you to handle.

BREAKFAST POTS

By flattening the base of your pinched bowl and adding a handle, you will find that you have made a cup. See if you can make a toy breakfast set, with teapot, cups and saucers, milk jug and sugar bowl. The saucers can be made by pinching out a flat thick piece of clay.

You could make the teapot by adding a spout and lid.

The handles are made with coils which is described on the next page.

After that you may like to make the jewellery container and lid shown on the opposite page.

2 Hold the clay in one hand while you press a hollow into it with the thumb of your other hand.

3 Work around the hole, gradually making it larger by pushing with your thumb and pinching with your fingers, making the clay an even thickness all the way round. Pinch around the top of the pot and neaten the edges.

Try not to leave your pot in between stages or it will begin to harden.

Egg-sized bowl

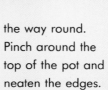

Add legs and feet

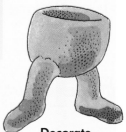

Decorate

Bowl

Add handle

Decorate

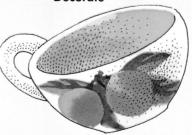

COILING

Coiling is another way to make rounded shapes like bowls and cups. The bowl shown in the photographs is made from plasticine, but you can use any modelling material. If you want your pieces to last, choose a firm, strong material like self-hardening clay or oven-baked clay.

MODELLING MATERIALS

22

1 Roll some modelling material into a ball, then roll it into a long, thin sausage, pressing evenly with your fingers.

2 Coil the sausage around itself, flat on the table. To build up the sides of the bowl, place the coils on the upper surface of the last coil.

4 You can leave the coils as they are, or you can smooth over the outside of the pot with a blunt knife.

5 After smoothing the outside, you could add more coils around the top for a decorative finish.

FRUITBOWL AND BEEHIVE

Make a model of a basket of fruit by making a large coil pot and then filling it with model fruit (see pages 24-25).

Turn a coil pot upside down and cut out a door and you have made a beehive. Make some bees with tiny coils, add some paper wings and skewer the bees onto the beehive with halved toothpicks. Hang some bees from threads above to complete the scene.

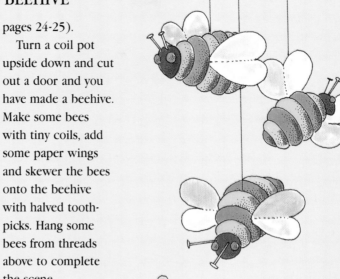

3 Continue building up the coils, adding further sausages when necessary. Make a strong join by smoothing well with your fingers.

YOU WILL NEED

- Oven-baked clay (or plasticine)
- Small rolling pin or pen or pencil
- Knife
- Varnish and brush (optional)

FAKE FOOD

Toy food can be fun to make – the number of things you can make is almost endless. Small pieces are best made in a modelling clay that is already coloured so you don't have to worry about a lot of fiddly painting when the pieces are finished. The plates of food and fruit and the vegetable pieces on these pages are made from oven-baked clay, which is ideal, but plasticine could also be used.

1 Start by making the fried egg. Roll some white clay into a ball, then roll it out to an oval shape to make the white of the egg.

2 Roll a small piece of yellow clay into a ball and gently flatten with your hand. Press the yolk into place. Roll out pieces of clay for the chips, bacon and mushrooms and cut to shape.

BADGES AND MAGNETS

Small models of fruit and other delicious sweet things can be made into fun badges to wear, or magnets to stick on the fridge. Model a life-size strawberry, a miniature banana or ice cream cone from oven-baked clay and cut it in half. When it is hard, stick a brooch back or magnet to each half with some glue.

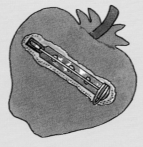

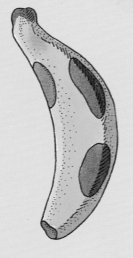

Roll out a sausage shape for a carrot and taper it at one end.

3 Roll out red clay for the tomato, cut out and decorate, make tiny green balls for the peas. Bake the pieces in the oven, and when cool arrange the food on the plate. Varnish to make it shiny.

Make a red and green ball and pinch in the top to make an apple.

Build your own burger with layers of meat, ketchup and lettuce between the halves of the bun.

Make grapes from little balls of clay.

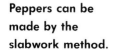

Peppers can be made by the slabwork method.

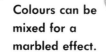

Colours can be mixed for a marbled effect.

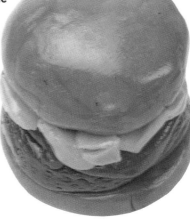

YOU WILL NEED

- Oven-baked clay in different colours (or plasticine)
- Small rolling pin (or pen)
- Used matchsticks
- Modelling knife
- Baking rack
- Varnish and brush (optional)

FLOWERPOTS

Tiny flowers like the ones here can look very pretty. The flowers on these two pages are made mostly by cutting and shaping flat pieces of oven-baked clay or by coiling.

Look at real flowers and try to copy their shapes in clay.

A MINIATURE GARDEN

Use the lid of a shoebox as a container for your own miniature garden. Roll out large flat pieces of clay for the grass and the earth, and then plant your garden with flowers, vegetables, bushes and trees. You could use a small mirror to make a pond.

1 To make a rose, begin with the tightly curled centre. Make a tiny sausage of clay, then roll it out to flatten it.

5 Make a green sausage for the leaves. Roll it flat, and cut into squares. Mark the leaf patterns with the knife.

7 Place the roses on a baking rack and bake in the oven. The roses may spread a little. When cool, varnish them to give them a shine.

2 Curl the strip of clay around a matchstick. The matchstick will become the stalk of the rose.

3 Now make the petals. Roll some clay into a sausage shape, then cut it into short, equal-sized pieces.

4 Roll the little pieces into balls, then flatten them. Press them in place around the centre of the rose.

6 Press the leaves into place underneath your rose. Make several more roses in the same way.

8 The white and yellow flowers have petals that are the same shape as the rose leaves. Put tiny balls in the centres of the flowers. Arrange them all in a pot.

- Oven-baked clay
- Skewer or thin knitting needle
- Cord or round elastic for threading
- Baking tray
- Varnish and brush (optional)

JEWELLERY

Making your own jewellery is fun, and can be much better than the kind you buy in shops. For a start, you can make exactly the designs that you want.

Oven-baked clay is best for jewellery as it is strong and light. Don't use plasticine or playdough because they are too soft.

You can build up a collection of necklaces and bangles made from beads of different colours and shapes, such as round, oval, square, triangular and so on.

1 To make the marbled beads, begin by rolling two different colours into sausage shapes. Twist the two sausages together.

ANIMAL BROOCHES

The shapes and colours of animals will give you lots of ideas for brooch designs. Details like cats' whiskers should be painted on after the pieces have been baked, but before varnishing. Make some earrings and a bead bangle in matching colours.

Use poster paint for adding details to your brooches. The paint will be 'fixed' by the varnish.

MODELLING MATERIALS

28

Moonlight earrings for evening wear.

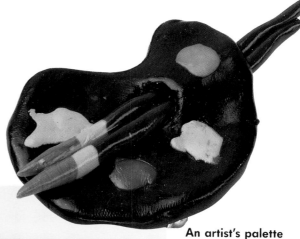

An artist's palette and brushes make an attractive brooch.

2 Roll the twisted pieces with your hand so that the two colours join together to make one long, thin stripy sausage.

3 Make another stripy sausage in the same way. Twist it around the first sausage you made, then roll them together as you did before.

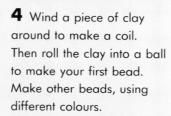

4 Wind a piece of clay around to make a coil. Then roll the clay into a ball to make your first bead. Make other beads, using different colours.

5 Thread the beads on to a skewer or thin knitting needle to make holes in them for threading. Bake them like this, without taking them off the skewer or needle.

6 Varnish the beads, if you like. Remove them from the skewer or needle when dry, and thread them together to make a bangle or necklace.

- Self-hardening clay (or potter's clay) and slip for joining
- Knife
- Poster paint
- Varnish and brush

PIGGYBANK

Here is a friendly, old-fashioned piggybank for you to collect spare pocket money. A strong material like self-hardening clay (which has been used here) or potter's clay is best for this piece because you want your piggybank to last.

If you want to get your money out without smashing your pig, cut a hole in the bottom and, when the piggybank has been decorated, slot in a piece of card to block the hole.

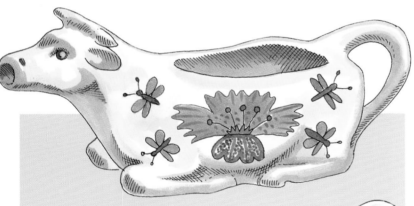

FARMYARD ANIMALS

Containers made in the shape of animals are more fun when they relate to what should be put in them. For instance, a hen is an ideal shape for an egg cup. For a milk jug, a cow is the right animal; leave the top half open, make a handle from the tail, and cut a hole in the nose for the spout. Do not use these for food, but display them as ornaments.

1 Make the pig's body first. Make two balls of clay the same size. Pinch out until you have two oval shapes of the same size.

5 Roll a ball for the head. Cut off one end for the snout and shape.

8 Add a curly tail. If you are using self-hardening clay, leave to harden. (Potter's clay should be left to dry and then fired). When hard, paint and varnish.

2 Moisten the edges and join the halves, leaving a slot for the coins. (For potter's clay, score the edges and join with slip).

3 Make the legs. Roll out some clay into a sausage shape, about the thickness you want the legs to be.

4 Cut the sausage into four pieces and shape into the pig's back and front legs.

6 Carefully join the head to the body. Then add some floppy ears.

7 Turn the pig over and join the legs to the body.

IMPORTANT
If you are using potter's clay, you must make sure that all the parts are hollow. If the model is left solid, it will explode when it is fired in the kiln. When you attach pieces make a hole in the body where pieces are joined.

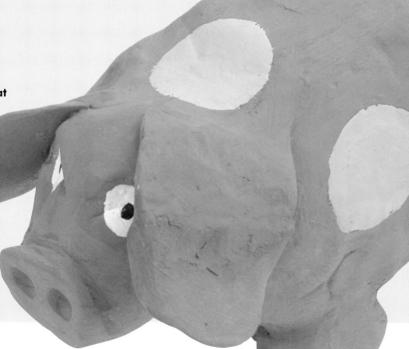

YOU WILL NEED

- Self-hardening clay (or oven-baked clay)
- Jar with lid
- Paint
- Paintbrush
- Varnish
- Silver stars (or glitter)

SNOWMAN IN A SNOWSTORM

This jolly snowman standing impressively in falling snow is quick and easy to make. Use a jar that suits the snowman's shape – a short, fairly wide jar will look better than a tall, narrow one.

When you have made your snowman, try making some other models in the same way.

1 Roll out the clay into a cone shape for the snowman's body. Tap the bottom flat so that you give him a good base on which to stand.

5 Add to the jar a handful of silver stars or glitter. This will be the snow that falls when you turn the jar upside down. Add water to the jar.

SNOWY CHARACTERS

Think of other figures you could make for your snowstorm scene. What else do you see in the snow? You could make a polar bear, or perhaps some penguins. Or you could make a Santa Claus, with a sackful of toys.

Using poster paint, add details to your snow-scene figures before varnishing.

2 Using the back of a teaspoon mould the snowman's neck, body and arm details. Shape his head complete with hat.

3 Roll out a long sausage for his scarf and flatten it with your hand. Press the scarf into place around the neck. Roll a small ball for the top of his hat and press into place.

4 Press on two balls for the eyes, add a pointed nose and a narrow strip of clay for the mouth. Leave to harden. Stick the snowman to the lid of the jar and paint as shown. Add two coats of varnish.

6 Turn the snowman upside-down and carefully slide into the jar. Screw the lid on tightly. Shake the jar (gently!) and watch the snow flutter down.

YOU WILL NEED

- Oven-baked clay
- Rolling pin
- Knife
- Scissors
- Varnish and brush (optional)

Turtle

SEA WORLD

The sea is full of all kinds of weird and wonderful creatures – why not create your own magical sea world by making some of the creatures shown here? Once you have built up a collection you could paint a sea background to display them on.

These models have been made from oven-baked clay and then varnished to make them shiny, but you could use any modelling material.

If you decide to create a sea background for your sea creatures, try painting it on card, with seaweed and sand and rocks and shells.

1 To make a shark, first roll out two balls for the body and the tail (the one for the body should be slightly bigger). Cut the smaller ball in half, and press the two halves in place to make the tail fins.

FARM FRIENDS

Why not make a farmyard full of animals? Colourful pigs, cows and chickens can be arranged on a background you've painted yourself. Make the farmer and his wife, too, to look after all your animals.

MODELLING MATERIALS

34

Sea-slug

Octopus

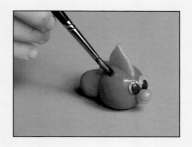

2 Roll out a flat piece of modelling clay for the shark's dorsal fin, and cut into a triangular shape. Carefully press the fin in place on top of the fish, keeping it upright and in the middle of the body.

3 For each eye, make one white ball and one slightly smaller coloured ball. Flatten and press into place. Make a ball for the mouth, and cut a slit for the jaws.

4 Bake the clay in the oven according to instructions and allow to cool. If you want your finished shark to have a slippery shine, you could give it a coat of varnish.

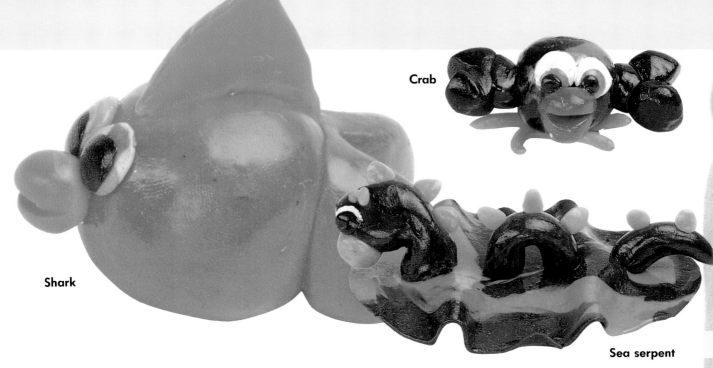

Crab

Shark

Sea serpent

- Potter's clay and slip
- Rolling pin
- Knife
- Pastry cutters
- Paint
- Paintbrush
- Varnish (optional)

LANTERN

This lantern is made using the flatwork and slabwork methods on pages 16 to 19. The modelling clay is rolled out flat, the shapes are cut out, and then the clay is joined together to make a cylinder with a base. Potter's clay or self-hardening clay are good for this model because you can buy them in bigger quantities, and they will make a good, strong piece.

1 Roll out a piece of clay. It should be about 25 cm (10 in) long. Use small pieces of wood on either side to keep the same thickness all the way through. Cut into a rectangle.

5 Bend the rectangle around and join the edges with slip. Smooth over the join, but do not attach to the base. It is separate to make it easy to insert the candle.

CUT-OUT POTS

Instead of cutting out a star in the side of your lantern, you could cut out a man-in-the-moon – to twinkle through the darkness. Or cut out a smiling face and use it as a pencil holder.

You could use the same technique to make a beautiful flower pot holder and decorate it with painted flowers and cut-out leaves.

2 Using the top of a jar or something else that is round as a guide, cut a base from the rolled-out clay.

3 With the pastry cutters, cut shapes out of the rectangle. When the candle is lit, it will shine through these holes.

4 If you are using potter's clay, score the short edges of the rectangle by cutting criss-cross lines with a sharp point. This will help them stick together firmly.

6 Roll out some more clay. Using pastry cutters, cut out shapes to go on the side of the lantern. Score on one side to help them stick.

7 Press the shapes in place on the side of your piece, using a little slip. Allow it to dry, then fire the two pieces separately. Paint and varnish if you like.

- Marzipan
- Slivered almonds (for ears)
- Decorations for eyes, noses and tails (vermicelli, silver balls, etc.)
- Food colouring (optional)

MICE IN THE KITCHEN

Marzipan is perfect for making edible models. You can buy marzipan in three different colours, or you can colour it with food colouring.

Marzipan is sometimes a bit hard which makes it difficult to work when you buy it from the shop. To soften it, keep it in a warm place for a while, or knead it with your fingers before you begin to shape it. Make sure your hands are clean before you start.

1 Roll a piece of marzipan into a smooth ball. (If the marzipan is a bit hard at first, knead it a little to soften it and remove cracks.)

3 Give your mouse a nose, eyes and ears. Colour some marzipan red for the nose and use small silver balls for eyes. Slivered almonds make great ears!

Make some marzipan food for the mice to nibble.

2 Shape one end of the ball into a point for the mouse's nose. You can either roll it to a point, or pinch it into shape with your fingers.

4 Roll out a strip of marzipan for the tail and press into place. Use vermicelli for the whiskers.

PARTY PIECES

Other edible shapes can easily be made from marzipan. Make small cars and trucks of all shapes and sizes to decorate your party table. Colour balls of marzipan with food colouring. Then mould the shapes, add little balls for wheels and headlights to complete the finishing touches.

- **225 g (8 oz) frozen shortcrust pastry, defrosted** (or make your own: rub 225 g (8 oz) flour into 100 g (4 oz) butter or margarine; add 2-3 tablespoons water to mix
- **Rolling pin**
- **Extra flour for rolling out**
- **Round pastry cutter** (or glass)
- **Knife**
- **Food mill or garlic press**
- **Decorations (silver balls, currants, or candied cherries)**

PASTRY FACES

Pastry is another modelling material you can eat, like marzipan, but it does not keep its shape as well. When pastry is cooked, it usually shrinks or stretches a little so you won't end up with exactly the same shape you made in the beginning.

When modelling with pastry, it's best to stick to simple, fairly flat shapes, like these pastry faces.

1 Flour a pastry board or work surface, and roll out your pastry. (Take care not to roll it out too thin, which may make it shrink out of shape when it is cooked.)

CHRISTMAS DECORATIONS

In some countries, people make specially shaped biscuits to hang on Christmas trees. You could do the same with pastry. Use decorative cutters to cut out the shapes, or make your own simple card shapes to cut around. Make holes for ribbon so you can hang up your decorations.

You could cut out the features, or you could use silver balls, currants, or pieces of candied cherry.

2 Cut out circles for faces, and other shapes for ears, hats, etc. Gather the leftover dough and roll it out again so you can cut some more faces.

3 To make 'hair' for your faces, press some of the dough through a garlic press. Dampen the top edge of the face and the bottom of the hair to help them stick together.

4 Press the hair in place. Add eyes, noses and mouths. Bake the faces in a hot oven at 400°F (200°C), gas mark 6, for about 10 minutes or until pale golden.

Cling film

Mixing bowl
(plastic)

Balloons

Chicken wire

Scissors

Newspaper

PAPIER MÂCHÉ

The name 'papier mâché' is French and means 'chewed' or mashed paper. Newspaper, water and paste are all you need and, on pages 44 to 45, you can find out how easy it is to make it. The two ways of using papier mâché, (1) by moulding paper pulp, (2) by applying paper strips in layers, are explained. The finished projects are usually painted using bright-coloured

Varnish

Brushes

Poster paint

Acrylic paint

Kitchen knife

Pastry cutters

poster paints – and here, you can have tremendous fun making up your own patterns and motifs.

On the next pages you will find some amazing projects to make. These include some very simple jewellery and Christmas decorations, crowns and masks for dressing up, and some beautiful bowls and vases, each with brightly coloured patterns painted all over the surface.

Wallpaper paste

Flour

PVA adhesive

YOU WILL NEED

- Newspaper
- Water
- Wallpaper paste (non-toxic)
- PVA glue

MAKING PAPIER MÂCHÉ

There are two ways of making things out of papier mâché – the pulp method and the strip method. The materials you need for both are the same. The best paper is newspaper because it soaks up liquid well. To bind the paper together, you can use PVA glue, a flour and water paste, or a wallpaper paste. Be sure to use a non-toxic cellulose cold-water wall paper paste. You can make up the exact amount you want which can be kept in an airtight container.

PAPIER MÂCHÉ PULP

1 Begin by tearing some newspaper up into very small pieces. Remember that it will reduce in size when it is soaked, so don't be afraid of using a lot. Place the pieces in a bowl of water and leave them to soak for a few hours so that they really absorb the water. Remove them from the water, and squeeze dry with your hands.

PAPIER MÂCHÉ STRIPS

1 To make a model using the strip (or layer) method, begin by tearing some newspaper into strips. Try to tear the strips all in the same direction. This will help to prevent the model from twisting out of shape when it is dry.

2 Do not tear the strips as shown in the picture above. Try to hold the newspaper so that you control the tearing, as in the picture opposite. For best results, discard any strips that have an irregular shape.

PAPIER MÂCHÉ

44

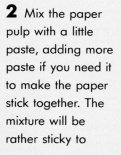

2 Mix the paper pulp with a little paste, adding more paste if you need it to make the paper stick together. The mixture will be rather sticky to begin with, but if you knead it for a while, it will become easier to work with. It helps to grease your work surface first, so that the pulp does not stick to it.

DRYING PAPIER MÂCHÉ

Papier mâché needs to dry slowly, and may take one or two days. Don't be tempted to put it near a radiator. The heat may make the model crack or lose its shape.

FINISHING TOUCHES

If you want, you can give strip models a thin, final coat of pulp for an even finish. Paint the models when they are dry. If you want to make them more waterproof, you can mix a little PVA glue with the paint before applying it; the glue will also give a shine to the surface.

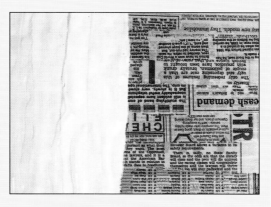

3 Soak the strips in a bowl of paste, then gradually begin layering them over the mould. Using fingers, smooth each layer carefully to get rid of any bumps or ridges. For a good strong model, you need to build up about seven or eight layers.

4 A good tip here is to use different coloured newspaper, if you can find it, for each layer, so you can see at a glance how many layers you have stuck down.

- Newspaper
- Wallpaper paste (non-toxic)
- Bowl
- Pastry cutters
- Petroleum jelly (or oil), for greasing moulds
- Safety pins
- Poster or powder paint
- Varnish
- Paintbrushes

BROOCHES

Papier mâché is perfect for jewellery because it is so light. These two pages show you how to make brooches out of papier mâché pulp, using different shaped pastry cutters for moulds.

You can make up your own designs shaping them with your fingers, but remember to keep your shapes simple for the best effect. And make sure your jewellery is dry before you paint and decorate it.

Simple designs make effective brooches.

PRECIOUS JEWELS

Collect 'precious jewels' to decorate your papier mâché jewellery. Sparkly beads, sequins or buttons can be bought from craft shops or found in junk shops. Pasta shapes, seeds and dried beans can be stuck to jewellery and painted. Use a strong glue, like clear adhesive.

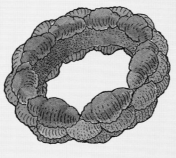
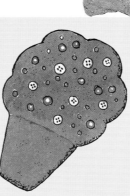

Try strong abstract patterns and add a touch of gold.

PAPIER MÂCHÉ

46

1 Following the instructions given on page 44, make the paper pulp. It should be soaked in wallpaper paste (or flour and water paste) ready for use. Grease inside the pastry cutters with petroleum jelly or oil. Fill each shape with some of the paper pulp.

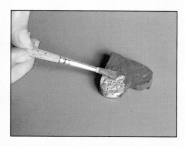

2 Leave the jewellery to dry thoroughly, then remove from the moulds. Paint the jewellery in the colours you want with poster or powder paint. You can paint on more colours when each one is dry.

3 Soak a strip of paper in paste. Use it to fix a pin to the back of a brooch. Add a few more strips to make it much stronger.

4 When the pin is firmly set and the paper is dry, varnish the brooch. Leave to dry.

Use animal-shaped pastry cutters as moulds.

- Newspaper
- Wallpaper paste (non-toxic)
- Silver foil
- Decorations (sequins, beads, scraps of paper, fabric and felt, etc)
- Thread
- Glue (clear adhesive)
- Eggcup

CHRISTMAS DECORATIONS

Making decorations can be part of the fun of Christmas, and if you really like the idea, you could make some to hang on a mobile or Christmas tree.

Tree decorations need to be light so that they won't weigh down the branches. Papier mâché is an ideal material to use because when it is dry, it is very light.

1 To make the silver wreath, first mix a quantity of papier mâché pulp (following the steps on page 44) and then roll it into a ball.

2 Gently flatten the ball into a round shape and neaten the edges. Cut out the middle with an eggcup, placing it upside down and pressing fairly firmly.

EASTER TIME

How about Easter decorations? Mould balls of pulp into yellow chicks. Give them yellow paper wings and red paper beaks. Use a real egg-shell as a mould for an Easter egg. Make more Easter things: hens, rabbits, and a basket to keep Easter eggs in.

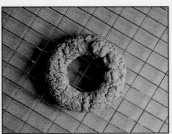

3 Place the ring on a wire rack and leave it to dry out slowly. Put it somewhere safe so that it cannot be knocked and get damaged.

4 Cut the silver foil into strips and bind them around the edges covering the paper mould completely. Press the foil close to the ring.

5 From your felt decorations, cut out two green leaves and a red bow and glue them in place. Glue a loop of thread at the back of the wreath for hanging.

- Card
- Masking tape
- Newspaper
- Wallpaper paste (non-toxic)
- Bowl
- Pencil
- Scissors
- Shiny coloured paper (from sweet wrappers)
- Glue (clear adhesive)
- Red crepe paper (for inside crown)
- Gold paint
- Paintbrush
- Paper fasteners
- Beads
- Plastic-covered wire
- Gold and purple fabric

GOLDEN CROWN

The crown on these pages was made from strips of papier mâché on a card base.

Use your imagination in thinking of different 'jewels' to decorate the crown. You could use buttons, as long as they are not too heavy; paper clips or metal curtain rings would look equally good. Instead of fabric, use a band of cotton wool around the base of the crown for the fur.

1 Cut a wide strip of card that is long enough to fit around your head. Tape it together. Cover with papier mâché strips (leave them jagged at the top).

5 Thread some beads on the wire and make loops at both ends so that the beads can't fall off. Bend the wire into interesting shapes.

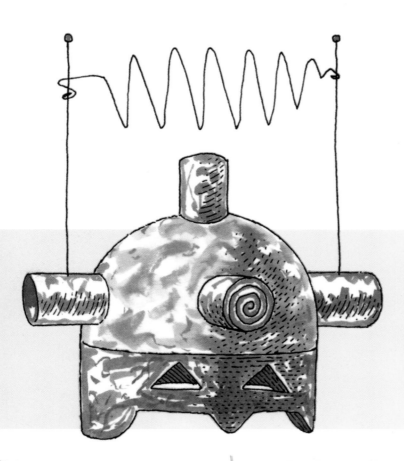

ALIEN SPACE HELMET

For the round shape of a helmet, cover a balloon with papier mâché (see page 58). Add a card rim with cut-outs for the eyes and decorate it with sections of toilet roll tubes, and wire for the antennae. Ask a grown-up to cut the wire.

2 When the crown is dry, trim the base and paint it gold. Because the paint is shiny, the crown will not need to be varnished.

3 On another piece of card, draw some 'jewel' shapes. They could be round, square or even diamond-shaped. Cut them out using paper-cutting scissors.

4 Cut out pieces of shiny paper a bit wider than the shapes. Fold the edges over the back of the card, and glue them in place.

6 Glue on the card jewels and attach the beads with paper fasteners. Crumple up some gold paper or fabric and stick it to the base of the crown and add some purple jewels. Fill inside the crown with red crepe paper for a 'royal' effect.

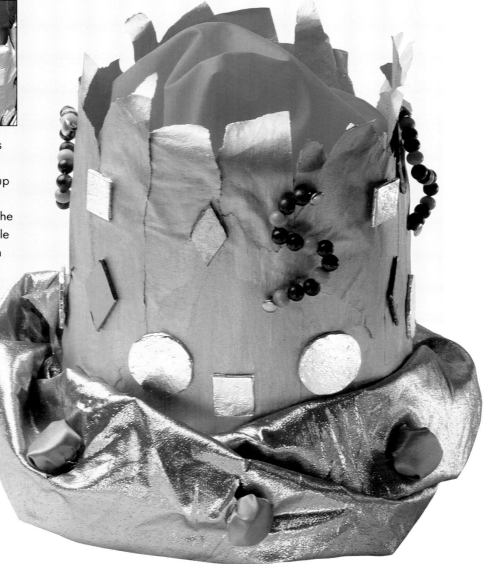

- Plasticine or playdough
- Petroleum jelly and brush, or clingfilm
- Pencil, scissors
- Strips of newspaper and white paper
- Wallpaper paste (non-toxic)
- Paints and brushes
- Elastic

MARVELLOUS MASKS

Masks are great fun to make. With a mask on, you can turn into any character or animal that you like! Masks are perfect for parties, and you can also use them when you are dressing for a play or pantomime.

Most of the masks here have been made from papier mâché strips over a playdough mould, shaped like a face. Follow the steps for the basic mask shape, and add your own finishing touches.

1 Roll out some playdough making sure that it is big enough to fit your face. It should be at least 2.5cm (1in) thick.

3 Remove the playdough mould. Draw the outline of the mask on the mould and cut it out. Remember to cut holes for the eyes.

Fire mask

Harlequin mask

PAPIER MÂCHÉ

52

2 Lay the play-dough on your face and gently press it into all the hollows and over the bumps so that it has the same shape as your face.

4 To make sure the mould is still the right shape, press the mould in place around your face. You may have to alter eye holes.

5 Brush petroleum jelly over the mould, or cover with clingfilm to prevent the paper sticking. Build up eight layers of papier mâché strips over the mould.

6 When the mask is dry, remove it from the plasticine mould. Cover with two layers of white paper to hide the newspaper print.

7 Trim the edges and bind with more white paper strips. Make a hole on both sides of the mask and thread a piece of elastic through it. Paint the mask in whatever colours you like.

ANIMAL MASKS

Why not ask your friends to come to your next birthday party dressed as their favourite animal? You could get together to help each other make the moulds for your masks.

You can use a round balloon as a mould for a curved shape, but it will not fit as well as a mask made on a mould.

- Vase (to use as a mould)
- Clingfilm
- Newspaper
- White paper
- Wallpaper paste (non-toxic)
- Sharp knife (for an adult to use)
- Paints in different colours, including white and gold
- Paintbrushes
- Varnish (optional)

COLOURFUL VASE

Many useful things can be made from papier mâché – even furniture has been made from it! The vases on these pages are made by building up layers of newspaper strips. They are very light and are quite strong enough to hold all kinds of different things – except water which would soak into the paper.

Paint and decorate them as beautifully as you can. You could even make paper flowers to go inside them!

1 Cover the vase all over with clingfilm to stop the papier mâché sticking. Cover the vase with strips of paper, building up to about seven layers.

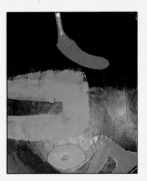

5 Leave the vase to dry. Then have fun painting your vase. Paint it one colour all over and leave to dry. Then paint patterns in bright colours.

LARGE MOULDS

Look for containers with interesting shapes to use as moulds. If they have complicated shapes it might be necessary to cut them and join them in several parts. If you are making a jug, you will have to make the handle separately. Cut a strip of card and fix it in place with masking tape, then cover with papier mâché strips.

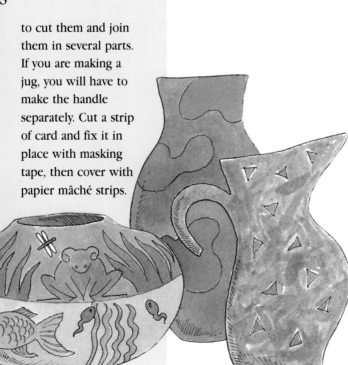

PAPIER MÂCHÉ

54

2 Add a final layer of white paper, and leave the papier mâché to dry. Ask an adult to cut the paper vase down the middle, using a sharp knife.

3 Remove one half of the paper vase from the mould, then remove the other half. Sliding a blunt knife under the paper helps to loosen it.

4 Put the two halves together again, and paste over the join with strips of papier mâché. Work all over the join until it is completely covered. Paint white.

Cover the surface of the white vase with pictures and words cut from magazines to make a collage.

6 As a finishing touch, outline the patterns you have painted with gold paint. Give the vase a coat of varnish to protect it.

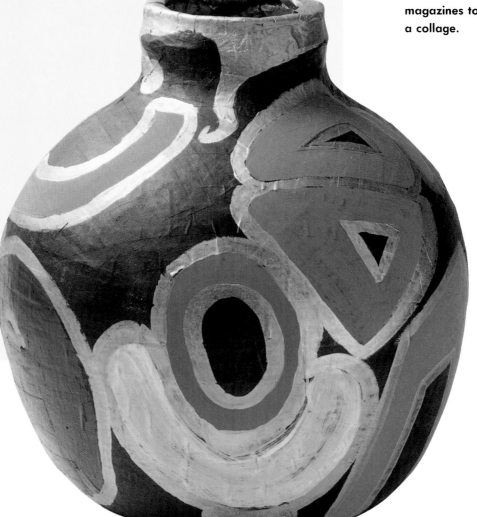

YOU WILL NEED

- Bowl (to use as mould)
- Clingfilm
- Newspaper
- Wallpaper paste and bowl
- Scissors
- Paints
- Paintbrushes
- Varnish (optional)

PLATES AND BOWLS

Ordinary kitchen bowls and plates can be used as moulds to shape your own papier mâché dishes which you can decorate in bright colours. When you stick down the layers of pasted paper strips press them down well so that you make a strong shape. You can also use pulp to make bowls and dishes.

Remember that papier mâché plates are not as tough and waterproof as ordinary plates. They should only be used for dry foods like biscuits or fruit. A coat of varnish will help to protect your plates and bowls.

TRAYS

Trays can be made by building up layers of glued paper strips in the same way as bowls and plates. Handles can be stuck on with tape. You could strengthen the base of the tray by starting with a base of card to give a strong framework.

1 Cover the back of the bowl with clingfilm so that the papier mâché does not stick to the bowl.

4 Now tidy the edge by trimming with scissors. You could cut out a zigzag edge, like the one here.

5 Paint the edge and the outside of the bowl in black. Leave to dry. Paint the inside a bright yellow. Add red flowers and finish like the bowl opposite. Varnish.

2 Lay papier mâché strips all over the back of the bowl. Don't worry about making the edges neat.

3 Build up about seven layers of paper, then leave to dry. Carefully remove your paper bowl from the mould.

IMPORTANT
When using poster paint, you will notice that it may crack as it dries. Try not to put the paint on too thick to avoid this happening. When dry, varnish over to seal the painted surface.

Make a set of bowls of the same shape and decorate them in different ways.

- Pear-shaped balloon
- Masking tape
- Newspaper
- Wallpaper paste (or PVA glue)
- Toilet roll tube
- Glue (clear adhesive)
- Scissors
- Paint (for head)
- Paintbrush
- Green and purple felt (for body)
- Needle and thread (optional)
- Pins

GLOVE PUPPETS

The heads of these glove puppets are made of papier mâché and the bodies are made of fabric. Why not make a group of glove puppets to use as characters in a favourite story? The puppets could perform the story as a play. To make a theatre use a big cardboard carton, with a square hole cut in front for the stage.

1 To make a dragon puppet, blow up the balloon. Wrap masking tape around the balloon to squeeze it up and create a snout for the dragon.

5 Cut the toilet roll tube in half. Cut slits around the top and fold flaps outwards. Spread glue on the inside and press into place. Paint the head.

A witch should have an angry look on her face. Make her a pointed hat and cloak from felt.

PAPIER MÂCHÉ

58

2 Mix up some wallpaper paste (or thin some PVA glue with water). Tear or cut the newspaper into strips, and soak in the paste. Then lay the strips over the balloon.

3 Leave the strips to dry, then cover with a layer of pulp. Smooth the surface with your fingers, then shape the eyes and the nostrils. Add extra pulp if necessary.

4 Leave the head to dry. Then cut a hole for the neck, about as wide as a toilet roll tube. Pierce the balloon with a needle and remove it through the hole.

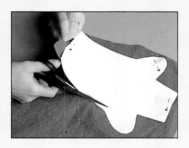

6 Draw a pattern for the body on paper and cut out. Pin it to the green felt and cut around it to make one side of the body. Do the same again for the other side.

7 Cut out a zigzag strip of purple felt. Glue into place along the bottom of the body. Sew (or glue) the body together along the sides.

8 Slide the head into the neck opening, and glue into place. Add the hands, the tail and the decoration on the front with more felt.

CLOWN PUPPET

Make a friendly clown glove puppet with a big red nose and wide smile. You could make the hair by glueing short lengths of wool to the top of his head. Remember to leave a hole at the back of the clothes that is big enough for your hand.

YOU WILL NEED

- Round balloon
- String
- Clingfilm (or oil)
- Newspaper
- Wallpaper paste (non-toxic)
- Weight (a small stone)
- Scissors
- Paints
- Paintbrushes
- Wool
- Glue (clear adhesive)

ROLY-POLY PEOPLE

These roly-poly people are great fun because they don't fall over when you tap them. The small weight inside the base keeps their balance so they just roll from side to side.

You will need to be careful when you twist the balloon to shape the body. You can take a pear-shaped balloon and use masking tape as you did to make the glove puppets.

1 Blow up the balloon. Twist it at one end to make a smaller ball, and tie with string. Cover with clingfilm (or brush with oil), to stop the paper sticking.

5 Join the two halves of the figure with small pieces of masking tape. Soak some more strips of newspaper in paste. Spread them all over the join so that both halves are firmly fixed together.

ROLY-POLY FAMILY

Invent your own roly-poly characters. You could make a whole family, including a chubby baby. Or what about a roly-poly shopkeeper – like the jolly butcher with his string of sausages? You can make roly-poly birds and animals, too, like the chick on the other page. Make the wings from yellow paper.

60

2 Tear or cut the newspaper into strips, and soak in paste. Cover the balloon with the strips, smoothing the paper down as you go.

3 When you have built up enough layers, leave the paper to dry. Then cut around the middle of the figure and remove the balloon.

4 Place a weight – anything small and heavy – in the centre of the bottom half of the figure. Fix the weight in place with masking tape.

6 Leave the figure to dry, then paint a clown face, arms and clothes. Tie some wool together in the middle to make two bunches. Stick the wool on top of the head to make the clown's hair.

Make this roly-poly chick for Easter.

YOU WILL NEED

- Card for base and tunnel
- Glue (clear adhesive)
- Newspaper strips, soaked in paste, plus extra scraps of paper
- Paints
- Paintbrush
- Sand
- Pieces of sponge

RAILWAY TUNNEL

Would you like to make a land-scape for your trains or farm animals, with trees, fields, rivers and rockpools and mountains? Here is a railway tunnel that you could make to go with that landscape. It's easy to put together with some card, some scraps of newspaper paste and paint.

1 Bend a piece of card into a curve, and glue to the base. Cover with the paper strips, tucking in extra paper here and there.

4 Now make some trees for the side of the tunnel. Take some small pieces of sponge and dab them with green and yellow paint. Leave to dry.

PAPIER MÂCHÉ

62

2 Paint the base and inside of the tunnel black. Cut pieces of black card for the front and back openings. Fold over on to the top, snip to fit and glue down.

3 Paint the tunnel green. Sprinkle sand here and there on to the wet paint so that it sticks. This will give the tunnel a rough surface.

Paint most of the sand dark green but leave some areas unpainted to make it look as if there are some rough patches of sandy ground.

5 Stick the bushes on the sides and around the base of the tunnel. Stick some little stones to the base and dab green paint on the front and back openings.

LANDSCAPE IDEAS

You could make other features, such as mountains with caves, or a desert island with palm trees. Make the main shapes of the land with card or crumpled-up newspaper and then cover it with layers of strips of pasted newspapers. Make rocks with papier mâché pulp.

Your tunnel can be turned into a road tunnel for your toy cars and trucks.

YOU WILL NEED

- Chicken wire (from hardware shops)
- Newspaper
- Wallpaper paste (non-toxic)
- Paints
- Paintbrushes (with stiff bristles)
- Pliers with wire cutters (ask an adult to help you)

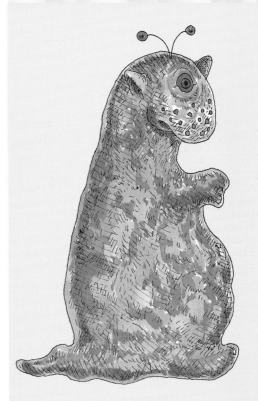

DINOSAUR

This dinosaur is made with both papier mâché strips and pulp over a chicken wire frame. You can make it any size you want.

Chicken wire can be difficult to bend into exactly the shape you want – you could ask an adult to help you but, if not, you may only be able to get a rough outline. This is why prehistoric animals are so good to model: they had all sorts of strange lumps and bumps!

When you make fairly large models, it is important to get a flat base so that they will stand up and not fall over.

SPACE MONSTER

Because chicken wire is difficult to bend into a neat shape, it's not ideal for really accurate models of things. But it's perfect for imaginary creatures that can look however you want! Try making a weird space monster, painted bright colours and with only one eye.

1 Bend some chicken wire into a dinosaur shape. Cut the wire if necessary to make the shape you want (for example, to make the legs).

2 Soak strips of newspaper in paste, and spread several layers over the body. Build up extra shapes, like ears and spine, with pulp.

3 When your dinosaur is completely dry, give it a coat of green paint. Paint the eyeballs white. Then put a dot of colour in the middle.

4 Dip a brush into some paint. Holding the bristles against your hand, flick specks of yellow paint on to the body. Leave to dry.

Cotton thread

PAPER

Paper can be used to make many kinds of models simply by cutting, sticking and bending it into shape. All you need are coloured papers in different thicknesses, scissors and glue, and some bright-coloured paints to decorate the finished model.

In the following chapter, you can read how to make a simple butterfly mobile, a

Coloured card

Glue gum

String

PVA glue

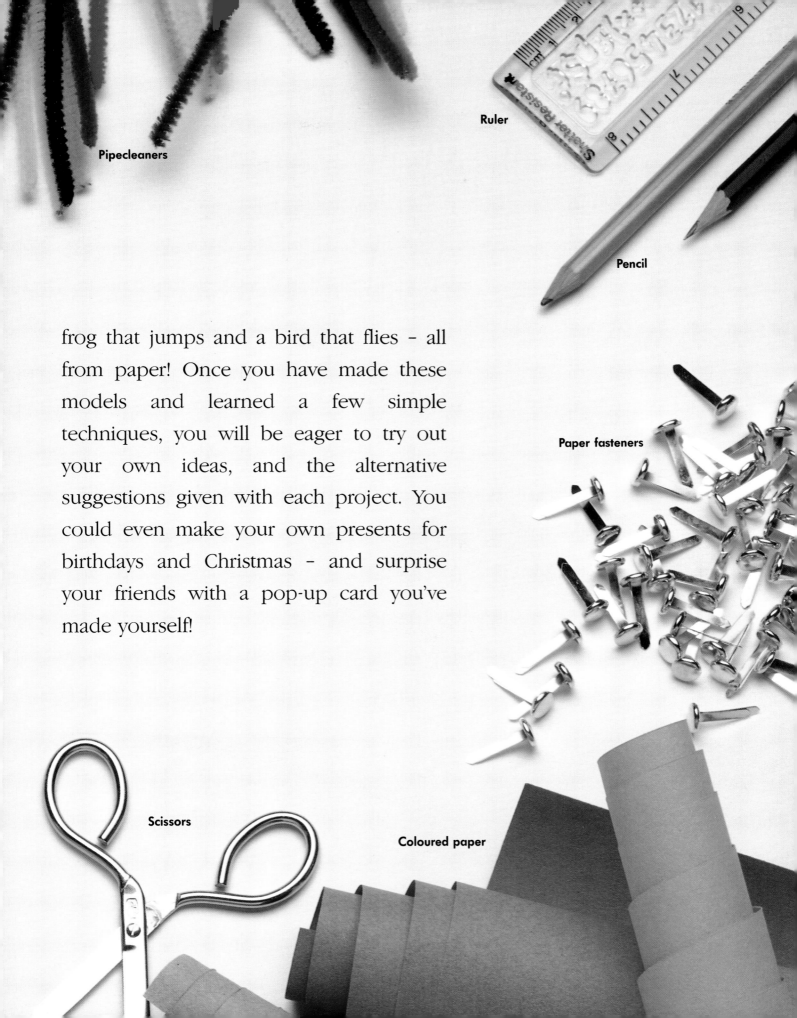

Pipecleaners

Ruler

Pencil

Paper fasteners

frog that jumps and a bird that flies – all from paper! Once you have made these models and learned a few simple techniques, you will be eager to try out your own ideas, and the alternative suggestions given with each project. You could even make your own presents for birthdays and Christmas – and surprise your friends with a pop-up card you've made yourself!

Scissors

Coloured paper

- Coloured card or stiff paper
- Scissors
- Glue
- Cotton wool and tissue paper (optional)
- Tracing paper
- Pencil
- Ruler

CROCODILE MASK

Large paper masks are great for parties, plays or surprising your friends! This crocodile has large, jagged teeth and flaring nostrils. It is made of plain, bright colours and simple shapes, but you can decorate your mask any way you like. The shapes you will need to make this crocodile mask are all in the box called Shaping Up. Paint on different patterns or add other paper shapes to make your mask unique.

1 See Shaping Up before you start. To make the eyes put shape D under shape E. Cut a slit to the centre of the circle. Slip one side of the cut under the other and glue down to make a cone.

5 Crease along fold 3. Then stick the eyes down. Glue tabs inside mask to hold the head shape in position.

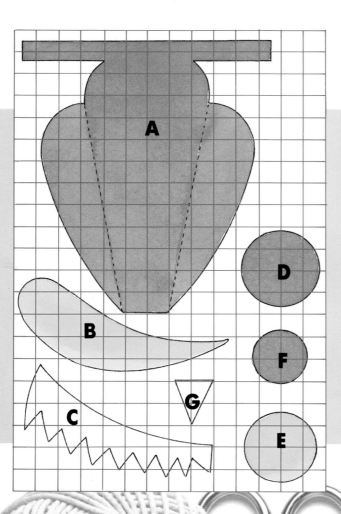

SHAPING UP

Following the instructions given on page 75, enlarge the design (opposite) onto tracing paper where each square equals 5cm (2in). Turn the tracing over on the light coloured card, and go over the outlines. Once you have transferred the shapes, cut them out. Turn the shapes B and C (the crocodile's jaws and teeth) over and cut round them to make second copies. Shapes D, E, F and G are for the crocodile's eyes, his nostrils and his two front teeth. To save time, cut these two at a time by putting one piece of card under another. If you want to make more than one mask, you could make a template out of heavy card.

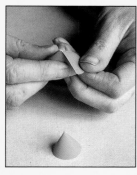

2 Make two more, deeper cones for the crocodile's nostrils, using shapes F.

3 Now make the jaws, by sticking shape B to shape C. Do the same with the other two pieces to make the other side of the jaw.

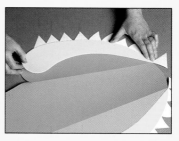

4 To shape the head crease along folds 1 and 2. Stick the two jaws down on the sides. Then stick his two front teeth (G) in the middle.

6 Stick the nostrils down right at the end of the nose. You can add cotton wool and shreds of tissue paper if you like, to make his nostrils flame.

7 Finally turn the mask over and fix a band of card to hold it in place on your head. You may need to try it on a few times to make sure it fits.

- Pipecleaners
- Coloured paper
- Pencil
- Scissors
- Paints and paintbrushes
- Needle and thread
- Glue

BUTTERFLY MOBILE

A butterfly mobile will flutter in a gentle breeze and is light enough to hang from almost anywhere. The butterflies should hang at different levels so make sure to cut short and long threads. Your mobile should also balance, so be careful not to put too many butterflies on one side!

1 Begin by drawing a butterfly's wing on one half of a folded piece of coloured paper. Carefully cut out, keeping the fold along the body.

2 Make some more butterflies using different coloured paper. Unfold the butterflies and lay them flat. Paint spots or whatever you like on one wing.

BIRD MOBILE

Make some more mobiles of things that flutter or fly through the air. You could make the wings for a bird mobile in the same way as you made the butterflies, then add the bodies and tails (stick them on with a piece of tape on either side of the wings).

3 While the paint is still wet, press the wings together again, then open them. The patterns you made on one side will transfer to the other so that both wings have the same patterns.

PAPER

70

4 Take some thread through a hole at the top of both wings ready to tie the ends to the mobile. Stick a short piece of green pipecleaner to each butterfly to make antennae.

5 Twist four pipecleaners together and make hooks at one end. Twist another one around them, as in the main picture. Tie the butterflies to each of the pipecleaner hooks to complete the mobile.

YOU WILL NEED

■ Card in two colours
■ Scissors
■ Scalpel (optional)

POP-UP CARDS

Home-made cards make very special presents. And pop-up cards are also full of surprises. Pop-up cards can be made with two pieces of coloured card, like the ones here, or with one piece of paper. Fold a piece of paper or card in half. Then cut into it at the fold. Try two straight cuts to pop out a square. Then be more daring and cut curves or jagged edges. Don't join your cuts together, or you will only have a hole.

1 Fold a piece of coloured paper in half and then fold in half again. Rub a ruler over the fold to crease well.

3 Ask a grown-up to cut along the lines with a scalpel, leaving the ends of the bands attached. Or you can do it yourself with scissors. Remember to place a spare piece of thick card underneath when using a scalpel.

BIG MOUTHS

There are lots of other animal pop-up cards that you can make. Think of other animals that have big

PAPER

72

2 Open out the paper. Draw wavy lines on one half of the paper about 2cm (an inch) apart, making two bands.

4 Insert a different coloured paper inside the cut, folded paper to contrast with the main colour. Bend the bands of paper to pop away from the card, and crease down the main fold firmly.

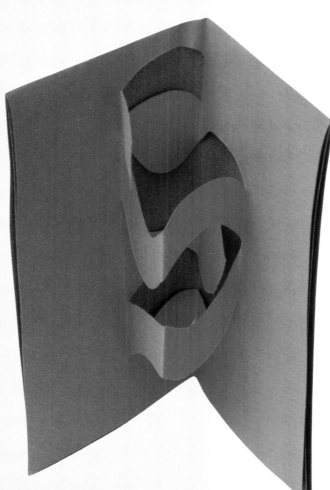

Try more complicated pop-up cards once you have made a simple one.

Make other pop-up cards with decorative shapes, then try making a simple, jagged cut for a mouth. With a black marker, draw the outline of a frog around it.

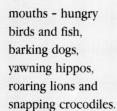

mouths - hungry birds and fish, barking dogs, yawning hippos, roaring lions and snapping crocodiles.

PAPER

73

- Card (for backing)
- Green paper
- Pencil and ruler
- Scissors
- Glue
- Coloured paper or paints and paintbrushes (for features)
- 4 paper fasteners
- Stick or plant pot cane
- Thread

JUMPING FROG

Have you ever seen a real frog jump? He may be sitting quite still one moment, then the next he springs up into the air on his long, bendy legs. The friendly frog here does the same kind of thing: just pull his strings, and watch his arms and legs shoot out! His legs and arms are all joined together by threads at the back and when you pull on one of them, he will 'jump'.

1 Draw the frog on the card (see the instructions below). You will need a head, a body, two arms and two legs. Cut out the pieces. Lay them on the green paper, and draw around them to get matching paper shapes for the parts.

2 Cut out all of the paper pieces and glue them to the card. You can cut out extra bits of paper to decorate your frog. White eyes can be coloured black inside. Light green pieces look good on the hands and feet.

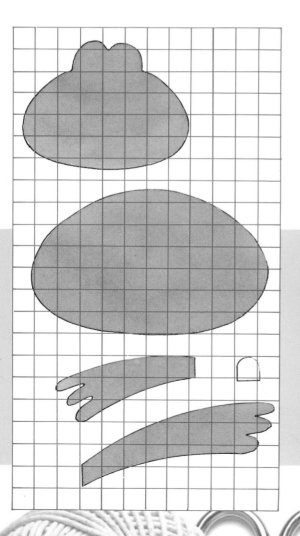

HOW TO ENLARGE A GRAPH PATTERN

To enlarge the graph pattern for the frog, start by ruling 5cm (2in) squares all over your card to make a large grid. Then copy the outlines from the small diagram grid shown on left on to your larger one, working freehand and finishing one square at a time until you have completely reproduced all the shapes.

Make other jumping figures in the same way as the frog, like this dancing clown. The legs and arms have two joins, so when you pull the thread, the lower halves will move separately.

3 Push paper fasteners through the head and into the arms to join them together. Open out the fasteners at the back to make them secure. Join the frog's body to his legs in the same way. Make sure the fasteners are all flat.

4 Glue the stick to the back of the frog. Tie a piece of thread between both arms; tie another between both legs. Tie a longer piece of thread to the middle of each of the shorter threads: the long thread is the one you pull.

cm 1 2 3 4 5 6 7

YOU WILL NEED

- Card
- Ruler
- Pencil
- Scissors
- Paints
- Paintbrushes

SLOT-TOGETHER MODELS

Many toyshops sell modelmaking kits made up of cardboard shapes that you slot together. These pages show you how to make your own kit – almost for free!

You don't need to stick to the shapes shown here. Once you understand how the idea works, you can use your imagination. The possibilities are endless.

1 Make a template from card: copy the shape from the picture above. Cut out the template, lay it on some card and draw around it. Do this as many times as you want, to make plenty of shapes.

2 Cut out the shapes you have drawn. For the slits, cut two lines on either side. Fold back the thin strips of card you have cut, and snip them off at the bottom. Keep the edges straight.

3 When you have cut out all the shapes, paint them. They look really good in lots of different, bright colours, like the ones here. You could try stripes. Spread them out and leave them to dry.

PAPER

STARLIT FOREST

Make a forest of slot-together Christmas trees. Draw the outline of each tree twice, then cut out and paint. Cut a slit in the bottom of one cut-out, and the top of the other. Slot your trees together. Try making stars to hang from strings.

4 Now slot the shapes together however you want. Add other shapes, too, like the tulips above. Cut a slit in the bottom of each flower, and slot the flowers on to long card 'stalks'.

ORIGAMI BIRDS

Origami is the ancient art of paper folding. Beautiful models can be made with very simple origami techniques. You will need to look carefully at the basic origami diagrams before you begin folding. Then look at the pictures to check what you are doing. Other origami shapes are fun to make, too. Why not explore other folding possibilities?

ORIGAMI FOLDING

Follow these diagrams to help you to understand the step-by-step pictures for making an origami bird. The dotted line indicates a fold. The shape of your paper will be the same when you make the folds in the right way.

1 Begin with a square piece of paper. Make a fold from corner to corner (a). The square now makes two triangles. Then fold the triangles in half towards the centre fold (b).

2 Fold the thin point of the triangle upwards (c), then fold it back again towards the bottom to create a small triangle (d).

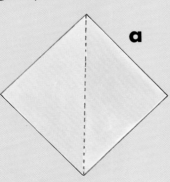

a

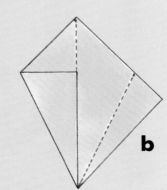

b

c

d

PAPER

78

You can make all
sorts of origami
shapes from a
square of paper. Try
it and see what you
can do!

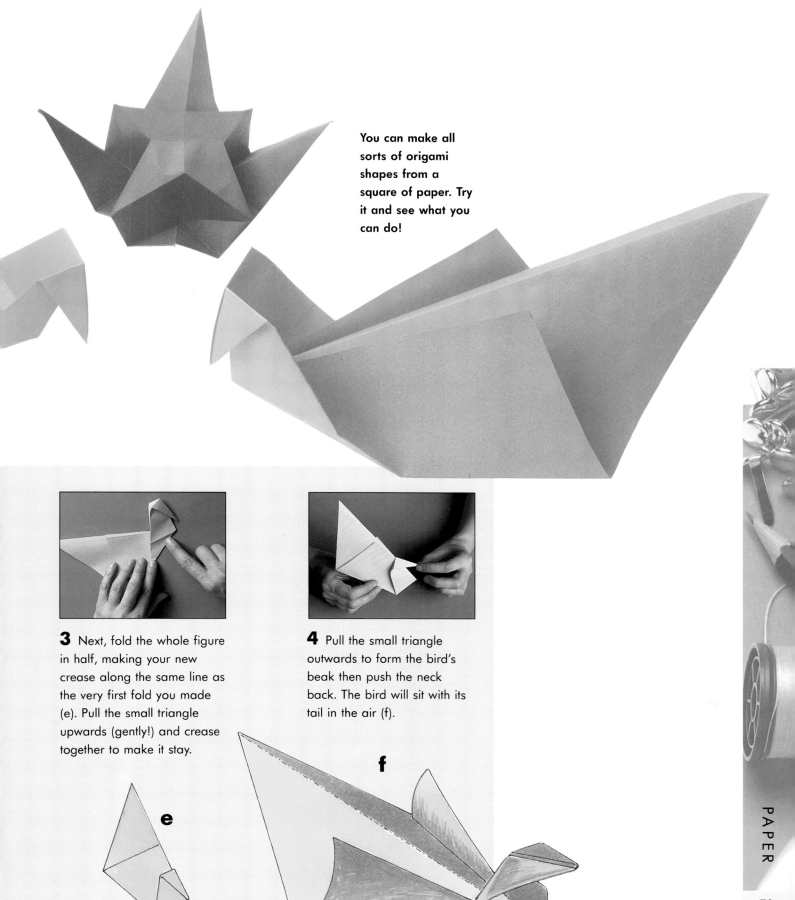

3 Next, fold the whole figure
in half, making your new
crease along the same line as
the very first fold you made
(e). Pull the small triangle
upwards (gently!) and crease
together to make it stay.

4 Pull the small triangle
outwards to form the bird's
beak then push the neck
back. The bird will sit with its
tail in the air (f).

e

f

Corks

Cottonreels

Buttons

String

JUNK

Junk modelling materials can be almost anything that has been discarded, from such things as corks and string to toilet roll tubes, egg boxes, cardboard cartons, squeezy bottles, jam jars and so on. Anything that can be built up using glue and paper fasteners into your own design.

PVA adhesive

Washing up liquid bottle

Scissors

Boxes

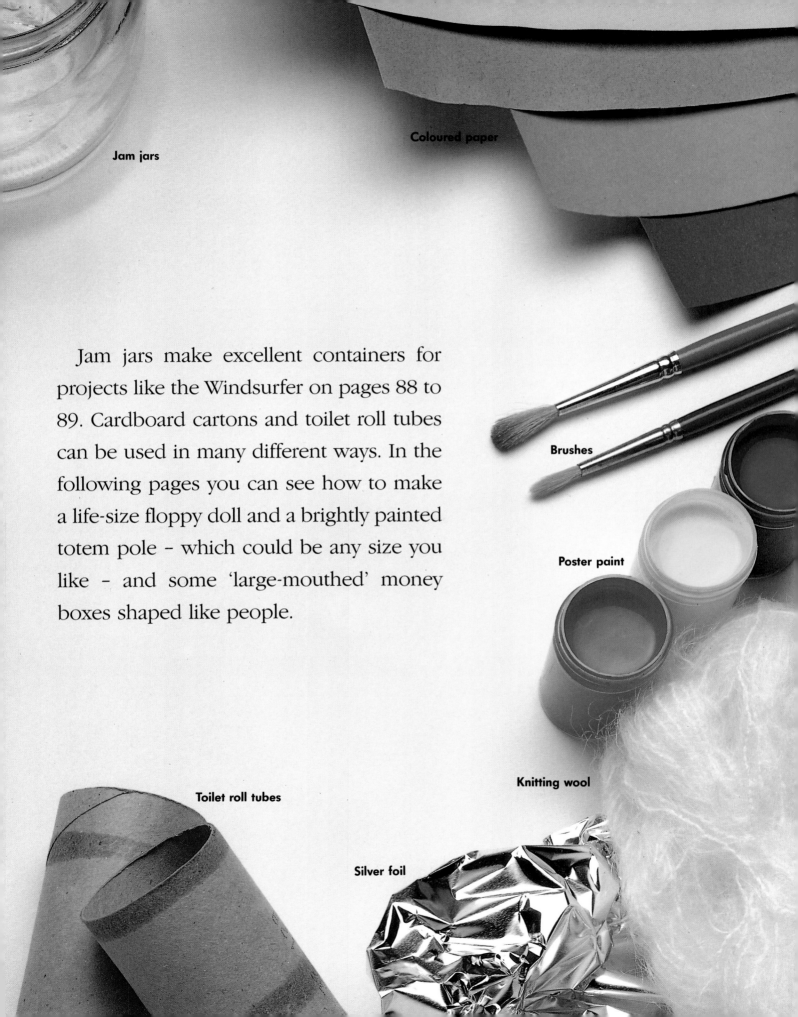

Jam jars

Coloured paper

Brushes

Poster paint

Jam jars make excellent containers for projects like the Windsurfer on pages 88 to 89. Cardboard cartons and toilet roll tubes can be used in many different ways. In the following pages you can see how to make a life-size floppy doll and a brightly painted totem pole – which could be any size you like – and some 'large-mouthed' money boxes shaped like people.

Knitting wool

Toilet roll tubes

Silver foil

- Cereal box (for body)
- 10 toilet roll tubes (for arms, legs, feet and neck)
- Corrugated card
- Paper in different colours
- Scissors
- Pencil
- Clear adhesive or double-sided sticky tape
- Stapler (optional)
- String
- Pipe cleaner (for buttons)
- Cork (for nose)

FLOPPY FLORA

Floppy Flora has arms and legs that can bend almost like a real person's. You could sit her comfortably on a chair in your room or let her curl up on your bed.

Floppy Flora's body is made from a cereal box and her arms and legs from toilet roll tubes. Corrugated card is best for her head and hands because it bends easily, but you could use ordinary card.

1 To make Flora's body, cover the cereal packet with paper and stick or tape down the edges. (Ask a grown-up for help if necessary.)

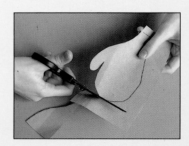

5 Cut out two hands from coloured paper, and one from corrugated card. Cover each side of the card hand with a hand made from paper, and stick down. Make a second hand.

8 Cut paper for Flora's hair and fringe. Cut into strips halfway up, and curl around the blunt side of a scissor blade (or ruler).

PATCHWORK PETE

Make a friend for Floppy Flora and for his clothes, use a checked fabric (one with lots of colours would look best). Wrap the fabric around the carton and stick it in place using clear adhesive or fabric glue. Give him masses of red hair, cut short all over. You could also make a floppy clown and pretend that he is the dummy and you are a ventriloquist!

JUNK

82

2 For her neck, cover a toilet roll with paper and stick it down. Mark the neck hole on the body, cut out, and slide the neck into place.

3 For the arms, wrap a piece of paper around a toilet roll tube: the paper should be longer than the tube. Stick the paper in place, snip the edges and tuck inside the tube.

4 Cover another toilet roll tube in the same way. Make holes at one end of each tube, thread some string through and tie the halves together. Make the other arm and the legs in the same way.

6 Make feet from toilet roll tubes cut in half, and painted or covered with paper. Make holes through the tubes and card and tie the hands, feet, legs and arms in place with string.

7 Bend a length of corrugated card around for the head, and cover with coloured paper. Stick the paper to the card with glue.

9 Stick on eyes, nose, mouth and buttons. Staple on the hair. Spread glue along the inside back of the head, and stick it to the neck.

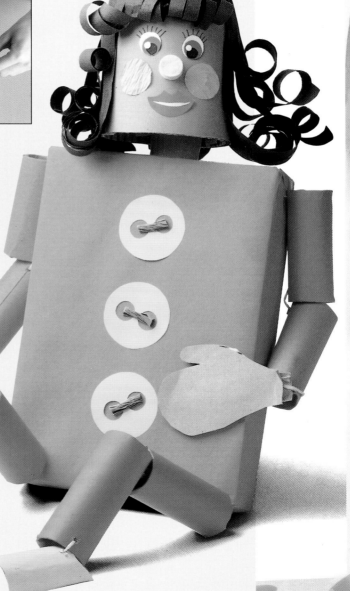

JUNK

83

- Cereal boxes and cardboard cartons
- White paper
- Scissors
- PVA glue or clear adhesive
- Masking tape
- Poster or powder paint
- Paintbrushes

TOTEM POLE

If you want to have fun making a really big model, try making a totem pole like the one here. Totem poles were originally made by the North American Indians. They were tall wooden columns, carved into the shapes of birds and animals and painted with bright colours.

CARDBOARD CITY

Make a modern city out of boxes glued together. Cut out windows and line with cellophane, or stick down silver foil. Raise some buildings on columns made from toilet roll tubes. Park toy cars in the streets for a realistic effect.

1 Glue the boxes together. Vary the size and shape of the boxes as you build your totem pole.

2 When the glue is dry, paint all over the boxes in a bright bold colour, and leave them to dry.

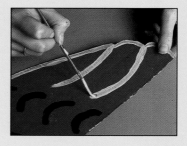

4 Paint the wings. When dry, outline the feathers in different colours. Now paint patterns all over the boxes.

JUNK

84

3 While the paint dries, make the wings. Draw two wing shapes on some pieces of card, and cut out.

5 Fold back a flap along the edge of each wing. Spread some glue along each flap.

6 Press each wing on to the side of the pole, and hold in place until it is firmly stuck.

YOU WILL NEED

- Toilet roll tube
- Card
- Paint and paintbrush (optional)
- Pencil
- Scissors
- Masking tape
- Scraps for decorating (paper, felt, fabric, wool, buttons, etc)
- Clear adhesive

HUNGRY HENRY

Hungry Henry loves money. Just pull the handle at the back of his head to make him open his mouth - and he will gobble up any money you give him! When he is full, empty him out.

Hungry Henry is very easy to make. All you need is a toilet roll tube, some scraps of paper or fabric, and a few bits and pieces to make his face and clothes.

1 Cut the toilet roll tube into two parts, one for the body and one for the head. The body should be longer than the head.

5 Paint the head and body, or cover with paper or fabric, and glue in place. Stick on eyes and nose, and any other features you want.

HENRY'S FRIENDS

You could make a female friend for Henry - Greedy Gertrude. Give her cotton wool hair and a flowery dress. And what about Peckish Petra (with red wool for hair), and Starving Stephen? Build up a collection of characters and collect different coins in each.

86

2 Place one of the tubes on the card and draw round it twice. Cut out the two circles to make a top for the head and a base for the body.

3 Tape the top and base to the head and body. Criss-cross the tape several times to make sure that the circles are firmly in place.

4 Tape the two parts of the toilet roll tube together at the back. (Leave the front loose so that you can open and close Henry's 'mouth'.)

6 Cut some pieces of wool for the hair. Spread some glue on Henry's head, and gently press the strands of hair in place.

7 Cut a bow tie from felt, fabric or paper. Stick the tie and some shirt buttons to the body. Stick a small strip of card firmly to the back of the head. Pull it to open Henry's mouth wide.

YOU WILL NEED

- Cork from a bottle
- Used matchstick
- Thin plastic
- Oven-baked clay
- Glue (clear adhesive)
- Jar
- Blue or green food colouring (or ink) for colouring water
- Masking tape
- Sharp knife (for an adult to use)

WINDSURFER

This windsurfer is a bit like the snowman on page 32 – except that he floats on the water instead of sitting in the snow. He couldn't be simpler to make from just a few junk materials and some oven-baked clay. The windsurfer here is very simply coloured, but if you want to decorate your model, you could paint stripes on the sail and a coloured wetsuit on the figure.

1 Cut a cork in half to make the windsurfer's sailboard. This can only be done with a sharp knife, so ask an adult to do it for you.

2 Cut a sail from some plastic and glue to a used matchstick. Push the matchstick a little way into the cork. Fix in place with a little blob of glue.

3 Model the windsurfer from oven-baked clay. Draw in the eyes and smile with a toothpick. Bake the figure in the oven, and leave to cool.

JUNK

88

SEA SCENES

Invent some of your own ideas to create a miniature sea scene: a sailing boat, a pirate ship with sunken treasure below, a lonely seagull or a mermaid on a rock. For the floating pieces you should use materials that are light and waterproof. Cork, plastic, wood and kitchen foil are all very useful. If you use paint, you should varnish it to make it waterproof.

4 Spread glue on the mast and under the windsurfer's feet. Carefully press into place. Let the figure lean against the mast and sail.

5 Glue some thread to the back of the sail. Tape the other end of the thread to the inside of the lid. This will stop the windsurfer falling over.

6 Pour some water into the jar and colour it. Lower the windsurfer down on the water, and screw the lid on the jar.

- Card for base
- Cardboard tubes, squeezy bottles, plastic tubs
- Foil
- Silver and gold paint
- Glue
- Brushes
- Black paint or paper
- Tissue paper

SPACE CITY

This wonderful space city is made almost entirely from bits and pieces of old packaging that you might otherwise have thrown away – cardboard tubes, plastic bottles and tubs, old pieces of card, and so on. The model shown here is just one way of making a city. You do not have to copy it exactly – think up your own idea depending on the kinds of junk you can collect.

1 Make the base of your city from a rectangle of card. Cut 'craters' from the tops of plastic bottles and glue them in place. Cover with foil.

ENCHANTED CASTLE

Make an enchanted fairy castle. Construct the towers and turrets using boxes and tubes. Make the stone walls by sticking on textured wallpaper blocks. Add colourful penants and attach them to the turrets with toothpicks.

JUNK

2 Draw the outline of a flyover on a piece of card and cut out. Use masking tape to fix it to two skyscrapers, made from a cardboard tube and a plastic bottle.

3 Cover it with foil and glue in place. Make other buildings from boxes, tubs and tubes. Paint them silver or cover with foil.

4 Make rooftops from paper or plastic cups painted silver, or gold-painted cones made from circular pieces of card. Cut flames for the chimneys from coloured tissue paper.

5 Paint or stick windows on to the buildings. Glue the rooftops and flames in place. Fix the buildings to the base with masking tape and paint over it.

INDEX